LIVING WITH DISEASES AND DISORDERS

Depression, Anxiety, and Bipolar Disorders

LIVING WITH DISEASES AND DISORDERS

Depression, Anxiety, and Bipolar Disorders

ANDREA BALINSON

SERIES ADVISOR

HEATHER L. PELLETIER, Ph.D.

Pediatric Psychologist, Hasbro Children's Hospital

Clinical Assistant Professor, Warren Alpert Medical School of Brown University

MASON CREST

Mason Crest
450 Parkway Drive, Suite D
Broomall, PA 19008
www.masoncrest.com

MTM Publishing, Inc.
435 West 23rd Street, #8C
New York, NY 10011
www.mtmpublishing.com

President: Valerie Tomaselli
Vice President, Book Development: Hilary Poole
Designer: Annemarie Redmond
Copyeditor: Peter Jaskowiak
Editorial Assistant: Leigh Eron

Series ISBN: 978-1-4222-3747-2
Hardback ISBN: 978-1-4222-3755-7
E-Book ISBN: 978-1-4222-8036-2

Library of Congress Cataloging-in-Publication Data
Names: Balinson, Andrea, author.
Title: Depression, anxiety, and bipolar disorders / by Andrea Balinson; series consultant Heather Pelletier, PhD, Hasbro Children's Hospital, Alpert Medical School/Brown University.
Description: Broomall, PA: Mason Crest, [2018] | Series: Living with diseases and disorders | Audience: Age: 12+ | Audience: Grade 7 to 8. | Includes index.
Identifiers: LCCN 2016053132 (print) | LCCN 2016053672 (ebook) | ISBN 9781422237557 (hardback: alk. paper) | ISBN 9781422280362 (ebook)
Subjects: LCSH: Depression, Mental—Juvenile literature. | Anxiety—Juvenile literature. | Manic-depressive illness—Juvenile literature.
Classification: LCC RC537 .B3373 2018 (print) | LCC RC537 (ebook) | DDC 616.85/27—dc23
LC record available at https://lccn.loc.gov/2016053132

Printed and bound in the United States of America.

First printing
9 8 7 6 5 4 3 2 1

TABLE OF CONTENTS

Key Icons to Look for:

Words to Understand: These words with their easy-to-understand definitions will increase the reader's understanding of the text, while building vocabulary skills.

Sidebars: This boxed material within the main text allows readers to build knowledge, gain insights, explore possibilities, and broaden their perspectives by weaving together additional information to provide realistic and holistic perspectives.

Educational Videos: Readers can view videos by scanning our QR codes, which will provide them with additional educational content to supplement the text. Examples include news coverage, moments in history, speeches, iconic sports moments, and much more.

Text-Dependent Questions: These questions send the reader back to the text for more careful attention to the evidence presented there.

Research Projects: Readers are pointed toward areas of further inquiry connected to each chapter. Suggestions are provided for projects that encourage deeper research and analysis.

Series Glossary of Key Terms: This back-of-the-book glossary contains terminology used throughout the series. Words found here increase the reader's ability to read and comprehend higher-level books and articles in this field.

SERIES INTRODUCTION

According to the Chronic Disease Center at the Centers for Disease Control and Prevention, over 100 million Americans suffer from a chronic illness or medical condition. In other words, they have a health problem that lasts three months or more, affects their ability to perform normal activities, and requires frequent medical care and/or hospitalizations. Epidemiological studies suggest that between 15 and 18 million of those with chronic illness or medical conditions are children and adolescents. That's roughly one out of every four children in the United States.

These young people must exert more time and energy to complete the tasks their peers do with minimal thought. For example, kids with Crohn's disease, ulcerative colitis, or other digestive issues have to plan meals and snacks carefully, to make sure they are not eating food that could irritate their stomachs or cause pain and discomfort. People with cerebral palsy, muscular dystrophy, or other physical limitations associated with a medical condition may need help getting dressed, using the bathroom, or joining an activity in gym class. Those with cystic fibrosis, asthma, or epilepsy may have to avoid certain activities or environments altogether. ADHD and other behavior disorders require the individual to work harder to sustain the level of attention and focus necessary to keep up in school.

Living with a chronic illness or medical condition is not easy. Identifying a diagnosis and adjusting to the initial shock is only the beginning of a long journey. Medications, follow-up appointments and procedures, missed school or work, adjusting to treatment regimens, coping with uncertainty, and readjusting expectations are all hurdles one has to overcome in learning how to live one's best life. Naturally, feelings of sadness or anxiety may set in while learning how to make it all work. This is especially true for young people, who may reach a point in their medical journey when they have to rethink some of their original goals and life plans to better match their health reality.

Chances are, you know people who live this reality on a regular basis. It is important to remember that those affected by chronic illness are family members, neighbors, friends, or maybe even our own doctors. They are likely navigating the demands of the day a little differently, as they balance the specific accommodations necessary to manage their illness. But they have the same desire to be productive and included as those who are fortunate not to have a chronic illness.

This set provides valuable information about the most common childhood chronic illnesses, in language that is engaging and easy for students to grasp. Each chapter highlights important vocabulary words and offers text-dependent questions to help assess comprehension. Meanwhile, educational videos (available by scanning QR codes) and research projects help connect the text to the outside world.

Our mission with this set is twofold. First, the volumes provide a go-to source for information about chronic illness for young people who are living with particular conditions. Each volume in this set strives to provide reliable medical information and practical advice for living day-to-day with various challenges. Second, we hope these volumes will also help kids without chronic illness better understand and appreciate how people with health challenges live. After all, if one in four young people is managing a health condition, it's safe to assume that the majority of our youth already know someone with a chronic illness, whether they realize it or not.

With the growing presence of social media, bullying is easier than ever before. It's vital that young people take a moment to stop and think about how they are more similar to kids with health challenges than they are different. Poor understanding and low tolerance for individual differences are often the platforms for bullying and noninclusive behavior, both in person and online. Living with Diseases and Disorders strives to close the gap of misunderstanding.

The ultimate solution to the bullying problem is surely an increase in empathy. We hope these books will help readers better understand and appreciate not only the daily struggles of people living with chronic conditions, but their triumphs as well.

—Heather Pelletier, Ph.D.
Hasbro Children's Hospital
Warren Alpert Medical School of Brown University

WORDS TO UNDERSTAND

biomarker: measurable substance that indicates a particular biological condition.

cognitive: related to conscious mental activities, such as learning and thinking.

externalizing disorder: mental disorder that is directed toward or disruptive to other people.

internalizing disorder: mental disorder that is primarily experienced inside the individual.

neuron: nerve cell.

neurotransmitter: chemical that carries messages from one neuron to another.

physiological: related to physical functions of the body.

reuptake: reabsorption of a neurotransmitter by the neuron that released it.

synapse: site where signals pass between neurons.

CHAPTER ONE

Teens and Mental Health

Adolescence is a time of incredible change. Kids transition from dependence on their parents to self-reliance. They seek new experiences, build deeper connections with peers, and experience strong feelings. It's also a time of physical and emotional upheaval, when overwhelming stress can cause problems with mental health. In some cases, these problems reach the level of a mental disorder.

The most common mental disorders among teens come in three types: mood, anxiety, and behavioral. *Mood disorders*, which include depression and bipolar disorder, affect a person's general emotional state. Depression is characterized by low mood, or feeling "down," while bipolar disorder involves unusually intense mood swings. *Anxiety disorders* are associated with excessive feelings of fear and uncertainty; they include phobias, social anxiety disorder, panic disorder, and generalized anxiety disorder.

Together, mood and anxiety disorders are sometimes called **internalizing disorders**, because they are primarily experienced inside the individual. People with internalizing disorders may feel anxious or sad, have low self-esteem, and not want to be around other people. On the other hand, *behavior disorders*, such

MAKING A DIAGNOSIS

For some health conditions, diagnosis is as simple as a blood or urine test. But there's no similar test to identify the presence of a mental illness.

Scientists are working to find biological clues (known as biomarkers) that will reveal the presence of mental disorders. For now, mental health professionals rely on the symptoms described by their patients, along with their own observations, to make a diagnosis. They often look for "the four D's":

- **Deviance:** behavior, thoughts, or feelings very different from those accepted within the society or culture.
- **Dysfunction:** state interfering with everyday life and activities.
- **Distress:** mental stress or unhappiness.
- **Danger:** potential to cause harm to oneself or others.

If several of these are present, it suggests that a problem may reach the level of a disorder. A fifth D, **Duration**, is sometimes added to clarify whether symptoms have lasted long enough to justify a particular diagnosis.

as conduct disorder, are considered externalizing disorders because they're directed toward or disruptive to other people. (Behavioral disorders are covered in a separate book in this series, titled *ADHD and Other Behavior Disorders*.)

How Common Are Mood and Anxiety Disorders?

Nearly half of all teenagers in the United States have been affected by a mental disorder at some point, so there's a pretty good chance that someone you know has one or has had one in the past. According to one large study, 32 percent of Americans between ages 13 and 18 have had an anxiety disorder. (For comparison, about 14 percent of Americans up to age 18 have had asthma.) For about one out of four teens with an anxiety disorder (about 8 percent of all teens), the disorder

EDUCATIONAL VIDEO

Scan this code for a video about the teenage brain.

It's likely that someone you know has an anxiety or mood disorder—almost half of all U.S. teens have been affected by them in some way.

has seriously interfered with their schooling, social life, or other pursuits and caused them a lot of distress.

Mood disorders are not as common: about 12 percent of teens have experienced either major depressive disorder or a milder form of depression called persistent depressive disorder, and only about 3 percent have had bipolar disorder. But mood disorders are much more likely to disrupt ordinary life. Depression severely impairs daily activities for nearly 3 out of 4 teens with depression (about 9 percent of all teens), and bipolar disorder causes major problems in the lives of almost all teens—about 9 out of 10—with the condition.

Half of all teens with anxiety disorders first experience symptoms by the time they're 6 years old, and half with mood disorders experience symptoms

Although we think of depression as being similar to sadness, it doesn't always look that way; especially in younger kids, depression is sometimes expressed as anger.

TYPICAL SYMPTOMS

Mood and anxiety disorders cause three types of symptoms:

- **Cognitive** symptoms are related to conscious mental activities like learning and thinking; they include problems with attention, concentration, and memory.
- Behavioral symptoms occur with both depression and anxiety; they include withdrawal, decreased participation, and reduced performance in work or school.
- **Physiological** symptoms are related to physical functions of the body. For depression, these include low energy and poor appetite, while anxiety tends to be associated with signs of distress, like sweating and a racing pulse.

These are just a few of the typical symptoms of mood and anxiety disorders. In the following chapters we'll discuss the symptoms in more detail.

by age 13. Because the symptoms are often subtle or hidden, they can be missed by parents and other adults—including the family doctor. Also, in younger kids, symptoms of anxiety or depression are sometimes expressed as anger and tantrums, which can confuse parents about the true cause of the problem. The longer the symptoms last, the more they can interfere with a teenager's development into a healthy, independent adult.

What Causes Mood and Anxiety Disorders?

We still don't know exactly what causes mental illness. In many cases, biological, psychological, and environmental factors are probably involved. The figure on

CHEMICAL SIGNALS

Within the brain and nervous system, billions of cells called **neurons** are constantly sending messages back and forth, coordinating all the different activities your body needs to survive. They do this mostly by releasing chemical neurotransmitters, which travel from one neuron to another at sites called **synapses**. After crossing a synapse, each neurotransmitter attaches to a specific receptor on the postsynaptic neuron, like a key fitting into a lock. Once a neurotransmitter has successfully bound to a receptor, it is released. It then returns to the synaptic space, where it is either broken apart or transported back into the original neuron for reuse, in a process known as **reuptake**.

Mental illnesses are thought to involve imbalances in the levels of neurotransmitters in the brain. For example, the amount of serotonin may be abnormally low in people with depression. The antidepressants known as selective serotonin reuptake inhibitors (SSRIs) work by preventing reuptake of serotonin so that levels are boosted.

page 15 shows just some of the risk factors that can increase the likelihood of depression, anxiety, or both during adolescence.

Brain chemicals called **neurotransmitters** are important contributors to depression and other mental disorders. Neurotransmitters carry signals between brain cells and are involved in many functions in the body, including mood, appetite, learning, and memory. If something goes wrong with them, there can be wide-ranging effects. For example, the neurotransmitters called serotonin and glutamate have been implicated in depression, while serotonin, gamma-aminobutyric acid (usually called GABA), dopamine, and epinephrine may play a role in anxiety disorders.

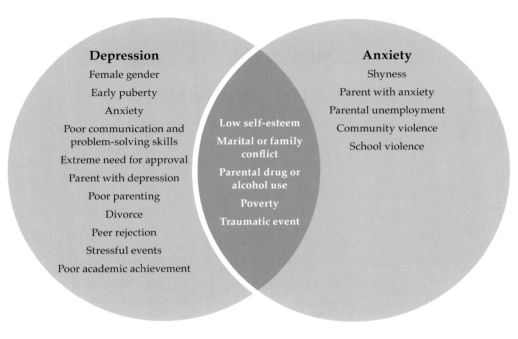

Depression

Female gender

Early puberty

Anxiety

Poor communication and problem-solving skills

Extreme need for approval

Parent with depression

Poor parenting

Divorce

Peer rejection

Stressful events

Poor academic achievement

Low self-esteem

Marital or family conflict

Parental drug or alcohol use

Poverty

Traumatic event

Anxiety

Shyness

Parent with anxiety

Parental unemployment

Community violence

School violence

Risk factors for depression and anxiety.

Text-Dependent Questions

1. How are internalizing disorders different from externalizing disorders?
2. What are neurotransmitters?
3. What information do mental health professionals use to diagnose a mental disorder?

Research Project

Compared with teenage boys, teenage girls are more likely to experience mood and anxiety disorders. Research a few of the biological, psychological, and social differences that are thought to put girls at greater risk for these conditions.

WORDS TO UNDERSTAND

anhedonia: the inability to take pleasure in normally enjoyable things.

delusion: a false belief.

grandiosity: exaggerated beliefs about one's own importance or abilities.

hallucination: something sensed that isn't really there—for example, an auditory hallucination involves hearing sounds or voices.

hypomania: period of high activity and energy that occurs in bipolar I or bipolar II disorder; less intense than mania.

mania: a period of very high activity and energy that occurs in bipolar I disorder.

psychomotor: relating to movement or muscle activity resulting from mental activity.

psychosis: loss of contact with reality.

CHAPTER TWO

Depression and Bipolar Disorders

Sometimes bad things happen. You fail a test or drop your phone in the toilet. Or worse—your dog dies, or your parents say they're getting a divorce. It's natural to feel sad, moody, or irritable under these circumstances. It would be strange if you didn't.

We all feel low sometimes, and we might tell a friend we're "depressed." After your grandmother dies, you may feel empty inside, but your grief probably gets less intense over the next few days or weeks. When you think about her, you may feel a pang of sadness, but you will also remember happy times you spent together.

In true depression, the main feeling isn't loss and emptiness; it's a persistent low mood and inability to look forward to things. Unlike grief, it isn't connected to particular thoughts or memories—instead, it's an overall feeling of misery. Depression often includes feelings of worthlessness and self-loathing, pessimism, and self-critical thoughts, as well as thoughts of death or suicide.

Depression causes problems with ordinary activities like eating, sleeping, and studying. **Anhedonia**, or an inability to take pleasure in things, means activities you used to enjoy seem boring or pointless. Even hanging out with friends might take too much energy. People with depression may cry a lot, have trouble concentrating, or experience physical aches or pains.

Doctors distinguish between several types of depression. *Major depressive disorder* continues for at least two weeks; on average, in teenagers it lasts about four to nine months. It may happen only once or return multiple times. *Persistent depressive disorder,* or *dysthymia*, is a milder form of depression that can last for years. Although it may not disrupt life that much from day to day, the ongoing feelings of hopelessness, low self-esteem, and low energy can have accumulated effects on relationships and the ability to deal with challenges throughout one's life.

Other Types of Depression

Several other depressive disorders exist. They all involve sad or irritable moods and feelings of emptiness, along with mental and physical changes that interfere with everyday life.

- *Disruptive mood dysregulation disorder* involves angry outbursts that are way out of proportion to the situation and not typically seen among kids the same age.
- *Premenstrual dysphoric disorder* can occur during the week before a girl gets her period each month. The depressive symptoms go away within a few days after the period starts.
- *Substance/medication-induced depressive disorder* begins during or soon after the use of alcohol, illegal drugs, or certain medications, such as oral corticosteroids, that can cause mood-related symptoms.
- *Depressive disorder due to another medical condition* can sometimes be identified from the patient's health history, a physical examination, or lab results showing a condition—including an underactive thyroid gland or traumatic brain injury—that can induce changes in mood.

One type of depression, called substance/medication-induced depressive disorder, is connected to drug or alcohol abuse.

It can be tempting for parents to write off their kids' mood swings as "typical teen angst," but those behaviors may be a sign of a deeper issue.

Moodiness or Bipolar Disorder?

The teen years can be a roller coaster of emotions—all that stress from dealing with parents and siblings, drama with frenemies, and struggles at school, plus surging hormone levels and a lack of sleep making things even worse. So it's pretty standard for teenagers to be moody. But some teens experience mood shifts that are beyond what's considered typical.

For people with *bipolar disorder*—which used to be called manic depression—extreme ups and downs in mood (the two poles in *bipolar*) go

MAJOR DEPRESSIVE DISORDER

According to the fifth edition of the *Diagnostic and Statistical Manual of Mental Disorders* (*DSM-5*), children and adolescents with major depressive disorder show these symptoms during a two-week period:

1. Either (a) a sad or irritable mood or (a) a loss of interest in or enjoyment of most activities for most of the day, almost every day.

2. At least four of the following symptoms (* indicates the symptom needs to happen almost every day):

   - weight loss (or failure to gain expected amount of weight) or either an increase or decrease in appetite
   - problems sleeping, or sleeping too much*
   - speeding up or slowing down of psychomotor activity, as seen by other people*
   - extreme tiredness or lack of energy *
   - feeling worthless or very guilty for no good reason*
   - difficulty thinking or concentrating, or inability to make decisions*
   - repeated thoughts of death or suicide

The symptoms have to cause distress, social difficulties, or other problems with daily life, and they aren't caused by alcohol, drugs, or other substances or another medical condition.

along with dramatic changes in energy level and the ability to think or concentrate. During mania (periods of very high activity and energy) they might incredibly happy, optimistic, or even unusually silly. Mania doesn't always mean "upbeat," though—some people feel very easily irritated during manic periods. Others have feelings of grandiosity, or exaggerated beliefs about their own importance or abilities. They might need hardly any sleep. Their thoughts race, and they may talk nonstop but get distracted easily. They often feel restless, have lots of plans for ambitious projects, and spend money impulsively.

During manic episodes, extreme mood changes occur every day, for most of the day, for at least a week—making it impossible to participate normally in social situations or in school or work. Mania can be enjoyable and exciting at first, but it rapidly worsens, causing unpredictable, risky behavior that worries others. Teenagers with mania often have delusions (such as grandiosity) or hallucinations that indicate psychosis, or a loss of contact with reality. They might even need to be hospitalized so they won't hurt themselves or others.

People with the bipolar subtype known as *bipolar I disorder* have experienced at least one manic episode. They may also have had major depressive episodes or mixed episodes (with both depressive and manic symptoms), as well as hypomania, which is similar to but less intense

RECOGNIZING BIPOLAR DISORDER

Unfortunately, even doctors can have a difficult time diagnosing bipolar disorder correctly. If patients complain about their low mood but don't mention their manic symptoms, they may be misdiagnosed with depression rather than bipolar disorder. Or the doctor may think that manic symptoms indicate another condition, such as schizophrenia, or dismiss them as typical adolescent problems. Other coexisting health issues, such as anxiety disorders or thyroid disease, can also make bipolar disorder even harder to detect.

than mania, without signs of psychosis. People with *bipolar II disorder* have episodes of major depression and hypomania but not full mania. In the milder form of bipolar called *cyclothymic disorder*, the symptoms are similar but milder: depression and hypomania recur for at least a year, but the depressive symptoms aren't as bad as a major depressive episode.

EDUCATIONAL VIDEO

Scan this code for more information on depressive and bipolar disorders.

Text-Dependent Questions

1. How is depression distinct from ordinary sadness?
2. What gives bipolar disorder its name?
3. What's the difference between bipolar I and bipolar II disorder?

Research Project

Many successful writers, scientists, artists, and performers have lived with depression, including such current stars as Lady Gaga and Dwayne "The Rock" Johnson. Choose a well-known individual from the past or present and write a short biography that focuses on their experience with the condition. If possible, include details such as when their depression was diagnosed, what difficulties it caused, and what helped them achieve their goals.

WORDS TO UNDERSTAND

adaptive: enhancing the likelihood of succeeding and surviving.

agoraphobia: a fear of public places that might be hard to escape from during a panic attack.

cognitive deficiency: impairment in the ability to do mental tasks.

cognitive distortion: an inaccurate belief resulting from the wrong interpretation of information.

compulsion: repetitive behavior or ritual.

obsession: a recurring and anxiety-provoking unwanted thought or thoughts.

CHAPTER THREE

Anxiety and Anxiety-Related Disorders

Everybody feels anxious sometimes. In fact, it's not unusual to feel a bit anxious every day, as different challenges pop up. Maybe you slept through your alarm and worry that you're going to be late for school, or you have butterflies in your stomach about a math exam or softball game.

Anxiety and fear are related, but they are not quite the same. Fear is a reaction to a real or perceived danger. If you're hiking and suddenly see a bear on the path, your body immediately triggers the "fight-or-flight" response: you breathe faster, your heart pounds, and the pupils in your eyes open wide. These and other changes are preparing your body for a confrontation (fight) or a hasty retreat (flight). Once you're out of danger, your fear goes away.

In contrast, anxiety is typically a response to a future threat. You anticipate that something bad might happen and worry about how you're going to react. You feel a vague sense of dread that you can't escape. If you're on that mountain trail and you jump every time you hear a twig crack because there's a chance it could be a bear, that's probably anxiety.

Anxiety disorders involve fears that are inspired by imagined, potential threats rather than real ones.

PHYSICAL SIGNS OF ANXIETY

Anxiety can produce the following symptoms:
- diarrhea
- difficulty urinating or having to urinate urgently or often
- dilated pupils of the eye
- dizziness or lightheadedness
- excessive sweating
- fainting
- overactive reflexes
- rapid or irregular heartbeat
- restlessness
- shaking
- tingling in hands and feet
- upset stomach

Anxiety is totally normal, and more than that, it's **adaptive**—it makes us more likely to succeed in difficult conditions. Anxiety helps by motivating us to do whatever we can to stop the future threat or minimize its effects. If you're anxious about leaving late for school, you can hurry to get there before the bell; if you're anxious about an exam, you're more likely to study hard. But if your anxiety is frequent, long-lasting, and intense, there is a chance you may be developing an anxiety disorder.

The Consequences of Anxiety

Anxious kids tend to worry about more things than others their age. They may be anxious in general, or only in particular situations—when taking tests, for example. They often have problems with memory and concentration. They experience **cognitive distortions**—inaccurate beliefs resulting from wrong

CATEGORIES AND EXAMPLES OF SPECIFIC PHOBIAS

Object of fear	Name of phobia
Animals	
dogs	cynophobia
cats	ailurophobia
spiders	arachnophobia
Natural environment	
heights	acrophobia
water	hydrophobia
germs	mysophobia
Blood, injection, or injury	
blood	hemophobia
injections	trypanophobia
injury	traumatophobia
Situational	
enclosed spaces	claustrophobia
bridges	gephyrophobia
flying	aerophobia
Other	
loud noises	phonophobia or ligyrophobia
vomiting	emetophobia
the number 13	triskaidekaphobia

interpretations of information—and cognitive deficiencies—impairments in the ability to solve problems and do other mental tasks. Some anxious kids get headaches, stomachaches, or other physical symptoms. They often withdraw from activities in an attempt to reduce their anxiety.

Unfortunately, avoiding anxiety-provoking situations means these kids never learn to cope with their discomfort, so the anxiety just gets reinforced. Anxious teenagers are likely to grow up to be anxious adults, especially if their anxiety is severe, starts early, or doesn't get treated. They're also at higher risk of developing depression. Untreated anxiety is often associated with self-esteem issues, lower grades in school, and dependence on drugs or alcohol as young adults.

Classification of Anxiety Disorders

Doctors recognize many types of anxiety disorders. What they all have in common is an excessive, irrational fear that interferes with everyday life.

Panic disorder involves recurring *panic attacks*, which are episodes of intense fear that start suddenly and for no apparent reason. They can include sweating, a pounding heart, chest pain, dizziness, shortness of breath, and other physical symptoms, which can be so bad they're sometimes mistaken for a heart attack. People may feel as though they're losing control or that they're going to die during a panic attack, and between attacks they worry about when the next one will occur. As a result, many people with panic disorder develop **agoraphobia**, or a fear of public places that might be hard to escape from during a panic attack.

Specific phobias are extreme, unreasonable fears of things that usually aren't thought to be dangerous, like elevators or clowns. For people with phobias, just looking at a photo of something they fear or thinking about being near it triggers anxiety or even panic—though they may realize it doesn't make sense. Avoiding what they fear disrupts their daily life, and when they don't avoid it they feel extremely uncomfortable or panicked.

Social anxiety disorder (or *social phobia*) is an intense fear of getting

EDUCATIONAL VIDEOS

Scan this code for a video about the differences between shyness and social anxiety.

29

Social anxiety disorder involves an overwhelming fear of being judged or embarrassed in public.

embarrassed, being judged, or offending others in social situations. Teens with this disorder aren't just shy; even a simple conversation may make them sweat or feel queasy, and having to speak or perform in front of a group can make them anxious for weeks ahead of time. They struggle when trying to interact with other people, which makes it hard for them to make new friends or keep the ones they have.

Kids with *generalized anxiety disorder* are constantly worried about ordinary things; they're often restless because they always expect disaster. Even though they know they worry too much, they can't stop themselves. Their anxiety makes it hard to sleep or concentrate, leaving them exhausted and irritable.

Separation anxiety disorder occurs in kids who are afraid to be away from their parents or other caregivers much more than is usual for their age. They may refuse to leave home or go to school. They have nightmares about being separated and may also have problems sleeping by themselves.

Obsessive compulsive disorder (OCD) is not officially an anxiety disorder but the condition does have many similarities to anxiety. It involves recurring and anxiety-provoking thoughts (**obsessions**), often along with repetitive behaviors or rituals (**compulsions**) that can't be controlled. These obsessions and compulsions take up at least an hour a day, every day, and interfere with daily activities. True obsessive thoughts are upsetting and unwanted, and compulsions such as counting or checking may temporarily help relieve the anxiety caused by those thoughts. People with OCD know that their thoughts and behavior don't make sense, but they are powerless to stop them.

EXAMPLES OF OBSESSIONS AND COMPULSIONS

Obsessions

- disgust with urine, feces, saliva, or other body secretions
- fear that a catastrophe will happen
- need for things to be arranged neatly or symmetrically
- excessive guilt related to religion or morality
- lucky and unlucky numbers
- forbidden sexual thoughts or images

Compulsions

- excessive hand washing, bathing, or brushing teeth
- repeating rituals (such as getting up and sitting down in a chair over and over)
- checking locks, appliances, or car brakes
- cleaning or other acts to get rid of contamination
- touching objects
- rearranging and putting items in a particular order
- performing actions to prevent someone from being harmed
- counting
- collecting or hoarding objects

A U.S. Army veteran displays one of the paintings he made as part of his therapy for PTSD.

Trauma-related disorders develop after someone lives through or witnesses a disturbing and dangerous event or its aftermath—like a car crash, hurricane, school shooting, or physical or sexual violence—or has been repeatedly exposed to harmful situations, as in military combat. They can also begin when a loved one is injured or dies suddenly. After these kinds of stressful experiences, it's common to be anxious, have nightmares, and keep thinking about what happened for a while. Most people gradually recover, but in some, the experience is too overwhelming, reaching the level of *traumatic stress*. Trauma can lead to two closely related conditions: *acute stress disorder*, a short-term condition that starts within a few days of the event, and *post-traumatic stress disorder* (PTSD), a longer-term condition lasting more than a month.

Stressful events that don't reach the level of trauma can also lead to difficulty coping. Big life changes like moving to a new town, starting at a different school, or being told that your parents are getting a divorce might trigger an unusually strong reaction. *Adjustment disorder* usually occurs within three months of the stressful situation and can include emotional symptoms like anxiety and depression, as well as difficulty sleeping and impulsive behavior.

Text-Dependent Questions

1. What's the difference between fear and anxiety?
2. How does performing rituals help some people with obsessive-compulsive disorder?
3. What kinds of events can lead to post-traumatic stress disorder?

Research Project

The "fight-or-flight" response to a threat involves a cascade of effects that begin in the brain and lead to the release of a stress hormone called *cortisol*. Describe the steps in this cascade.

WORDS TO UNDERSTAND

black box warning: the most serious type of drug-related warning issued by the U.S. Food and Drug Administration (FDA).

psychotherapy: talk therapy.

psychotropic: affecting the mind.

remission: a period when an illness causes few or no symptoms.

side effect: an unwanted effect of taking a drug.

CHAPTER FOUR

Treatment of Mood and Anxiety Disorders

When a patient begins seeing a therapist for a mental disorder, the therapist typically puts together a treatment plan based on the patient's specific situation. Effective treatment often includes psychotherapy, medication, or a combination of the two, depending on the severity of the disorder.

Psychotherapy

Psychotherapy is designed to help you understand your feelings and deal with them better. By working with a trained therapist, you can learn strategies for changing unhealthy ways of thinking and for coping with problems. You can talk to your therapist about anything—your thoughts and feelings, bad experiences at school, fights with your friends or parents—in a safe, supportive, and confidential environment. It can be upsetting to discuss some topics, but the more honest and open you are, the better your therapist can understand what you're going through and help you get better.

In many cases, psychotherapy consists of *individual therapy*, with one-on-one sessions between a patient and therapist. It can sometimes be helpful to include parents and other family members in the process—especially when the patient's condition has disturbed their mental well-being or when the family dynamic makes the disorder worse. *Family therapy* teaches participants how to communicate and act more supportively toward each other.

Another option is *group therapy*, where multiple patients participate along with one or more therapists. In some ways, group therapy can be even better for teens than one-on-one sessions. Talking with people your own age can make you feel less isolated, and hearing about their successes can show you that there's light at the end of the tunnel. If you're shy, the group environment gives you a safe place to practice your social skills.

Other Types of Psychotherapy

Because every patient is different, a trained therapist will decide which to use based on each individual's needs.

Cognitive-behavioral therapy (CBT) is one of the most common types of talk therapy used with teens. It's a combination of cognitive therapy, which looks at problems with the patient's thinking, and behavioral therapy, which targets unhealthy actions. During CBT, the therapist helps you explore your patterns of thinking, recognize when they are distorted and unhelpful, and adjust your beliefs so you can actively change your behavior.

CBT is especially effective in people with depression, who usually have negative thought patterns that affect the way they interact with others and think about their situation. And CBT can help people with bipolar disorder deal with their symptoms, learn how to recognize when they're about to have a mood swing, and stay on their medication.

TYPES OF MENTAL HEALTH SPECIALISTS

Many different kinds of professionals can help people with mental disorders. In general, they have all had training in human behavior and psychotherapy, as well as supervised experience working with patients before being certified to practice. They must pass an examination in order to be licensed by the state where they work.

Psychiatrists are physicians who specialize in the diagnosis and treatment of emotional and behavioral disorders. Child and adolescent psychiatrists have specific training in problems that affect young people, such as learning disabilities and autism spectrum disorders. All psychiatrists can prescribe medications, but not all provide psychotherapy.

Psychologists go to graduate school to study psychology and usually have a doctoral degree. Because they are not medical doctors, they typically can't prescribe medications, but they can refer patients to another provider if necessary.

Social workers earn a graduate degree in social work, which usually requires on-the-job experience at community agencies. Their training focuses on counseling. They also help people access services available within their community.

One type of CBT is called *exposure therapy*. This approach helps patients confront their fears or unpleasant memories gradually, in a safe environment. First, the therapist helps the patient identify things that trigger anxiety and rate

Exposure therapy for someone with cynophobia (fear of dogs) might progress very gradually—from talking about dogs, to looking at photos, to watching videos, to finally meeting a friendly puppy.

how hard they would be to face. For instance, if a patient has a fear of cats, the therapist might expose the patient to a mild trigger (such as a picture or video of a cat) and help her through the experience until she's no longer anxious. They can then move on to a trigger that is slightly scarier. Eventually they confront—and conquer—the most extreme trigger. Exposure therapy can help patients with phobias, obsessive-compulsive disorder, or PTSD, giving them tools to reduce their reaction to anxiety triggers.

Interpersonal therapy (IPT) focuses on relationships. It looks at how the way patients communicate and interact with others affects their emotional state. Using IPT, a therapist helps patients look at past and current social interactions and try to understand how negative behaviors cause problems.

Medication

Psychotropic drugs are medications that work on your mind. They are believed to improve the balance of chemicals in your brain that influence your mood and behavior. Psychotropic drugs don't cure mental disorders, but ideally they lead to **remission**, in which all signs of the mental disorder disappear. Even if some symptoms continue, medication can help you feel better and enjoy your life.

EDUCATIONAL VIDEO

Scan this code for a video about treatment plans.

No drug helps every patient, which is why many treatment options exist for some conditions. Also, all medications are associated with **side effects**, or unwanted effects that occur along with the intended ones. Just like the benefits of a given drug, the side effects vary from patient to patient. That's why multiple medications may be tried, as well as different doses, before patients find one that works and that they can tolerate. If you start taking a medication to help your mental health, you should be monitored to ensure that you don't have a bad reaction. Listed here are different types of psychotropic medications:

- **Antidepressants.** Dozens of drugs are available to treat depression. They work by altering the levels of one or more brain chemicals involved in emotions, such as serotonin, norepinephrine, and dopamine. The first medication prescribed for teenagers with depression is often one of the selective serotonin reuptake inhibitors (or SSRIs), such as fluoxetine (brand name Prozac) or escitalopram (Lexapro), because they generally don't cause serious side effects and can be taken just once a day. Other types of medication may be tried, such as a serotonin-norepinephrine reuptake inhibitor (SNRI) and antidepressants called tricyclics.

- **Anti-anxiety medications.** Most commonly, anxiety disorders in teenagers are treated using SSRIs or other antidepressants. Certain medications given to adults, such as benzodiazepines and antihistamines, tend to be avoided but are sometimes used briefly for teens with severe anxiety.
- **Mood stabilizers and anticonvulsant medications.** These are often used to treat patients with bipolar disorder. Lithium is the best-known mood stabilizer. Unlike most drugs prescribed to treat mental disorders,

WARNING ABOUT ANTIDEPRESSANTS

In 2004, the U.S. Food and Drug Administration (FDA) began warning the public about an increased risk of suicidal thoughts or actions in children and teenagers who recently started treatment with antidepressant medication. It issued its most serious type of warning, a black box warning, which had to be included in the product labeling for all antidepressants. In 2007 the warning was extended to include young adults aged 18 to 24.

A review of studies supported by the National Institute of Mental Health found that the benefits of antidepressant treatment are likely to outweigh the risks. Still, the FDA emphasizes that young patients should be monitored and closely observed during treatment.

If your depression has gotten worse since you started taking an antidepressant, or if you've started thinking about suicide, tell your parents or other trusted adult immediately, as well as the doctor who prescribed the medication. Stopping medication abruptly can cause other symptoms, so keep taking your antidepressant until you consult your doctor, and follow his or her instructions on how to stop if necessary.

lithium occurs in nature. Most of the lithium used by Americans is mined out of dry lakes in Argentina and Chile. Anticonvulsants were originally used to prevent seizures, such as in patients with epilepsy. But they are sometimes they used to treat bipolar disorder in teenagers.

- **Antipsychotics.** Sometimes antipsychotic medications are used to control delusions and hallucinations, which occur in some patients with bipolar disorder, as well as severe anxiety. The oldest ones, which are known as first-generation or "typical" antipsychotics, work by blocking the binding of dopamine to its receptors. Newer, second-generation ("atypical" or novel) antipsychotics are used more often because their side effects (which include weight gain and diabetes) are easier to tolerate. Atypical antipsychotics block the binding of both dopamine and serotonin to their receptors.

Support Groups

Living with a mental disorder can be lonely. Participating in a support group is one way to feel less isolated. Meeting in person with peers who are going through similar experiences can encourage you to feel positive about your own future. Check the online listings of the Anxiety and Depression Association of America (www.adaa.org/finding-help/getting-support) and the National Mental Health Consumers' Self-Help Clearinghouse (www.mhselfhelp.org) for a support group in your area. Local affiliates of Mental Health America (www.mentalhealthamerica.net) can also be helpful resources.

If a support group that fits your needs isn't available near you, look for one that meets online, such as the young adult support group from the Depression and Bipolar Support Alliance. These groups are led by others with mood disorders rather than by mental health professionals. You can actively participate or just listen without giving your real name if you prefer. Online communities like oktotalk.org are also places where you can share stories and get support from people your own age.

ELECTROCONVULSIVE THERAPY

Some people with severe depression don't respond to psychotherapy and medication. For these individuals, a treatment known as electroconvulsive therapy (ECT) can make a dramatic difference. ECT sends an electrical current through the patient's brain to cause a short seizure (usually lasting less than a minute), which produces chemical changes that reduce depression. Patients sleep through the entire procedure, so they don't feel any pain. They wake up shortly afterward and recover in about an hour. Long ago, "shock therapy" was often misused and done without anesthesia; as a result ECT is still controversial among the general public. But as it's done today, ECT doesn't deserve its bad reputation. It can be a literal lifesaver for some patients.

Complementary Health Approaches

Some people try nontraditional treatments to improve their mental health. These can be incorporated into a treatment plan along with more conventional methods, such as psychotherapy and medication. However, many of them haven't been carefully studied as treatments for anxiety or mood disorders. Before you try any of the complementary health approach, discuss it with your doctor.

- **Natural products.** Herbs, vitamins, minerals, and probiotics (foods or products containing live microorganisms) are one popular type of complementary health approach. Although many people believe they work, research doesn't always back them up. More well-designed studies are needed to confirm which natural products are safe and worth trying.

- **Mind and body practices.** These practices, such as meditation and yoga, are based on the idea that the interactions between our minds and our bodies can affect our health and well-being. Meditation is a type of thinking performed to increase relaxation and calmness. It's usually done in a quiet place while concentrating on the sensation of breathing or on particular words or objects. Yoga usually combines attention to breathing along with physical poses. Many people use it to improve their strength, balance, and flexibility, but it can also help reduce stress and combat anxiety and depression.

- **Self-help phone apps.** Mental health apps let you use your smartphone to track your moods, practice breathing techniques to manage stress, or reinforce the tools you've learned during therapy. A good place to start looking for apps is the Anxiety and Depression Association of America website, which has app reviews written by mental health professionals.

Text-Dependent Questions

1. What are one advantage and one disadvantage of group therapy compared with individual therapy?
2. In the United States, what government agency decides whether a drug should be approved for use?
3. What are some complementary health approaches to depression and anxiety?

Research Project

Choose one type of antidepressant to research. Write a description of its mechanism of action, the main side effects, and any other information you think someone should know before taking that medication.

WORDS TO UNDERSTAND

carbohydrates: energy-rich compounds (such as sugars and starches) that, along with protein and fat, are one of the main types of nutrients in food.

melatonin: a substance that signals our bodies when it's time to go to sleep.

resilience: the ability to bounce back from difficult situations.

CHAPTER FIVE

Facing the Challenges of Mood and Anxiety Disorders

Having good mental health starts with taking care of yourself—and that includes making sure you're physically healthy. Eating right, exercising regularly, and getting a good night's sleep are all important parts of feeling your best.

Nutrition

At the most basic level, the food you consume gives your body the energy and nutrients it needs to function. When you eat a balanced diet, you're setting yourself up to feel strong both physically and mentally. Although a single way of eating doesn't work well for everybody, here are some general suggestions that might help your mood and overall mental health:

- **Eat breakfast.** Even if you're not hungry when you get up, try eating something high in protein, like yogurt or a hard-boiled egg, to give you energy and prevent you from crashing mid-morning.
- **Eat regularly.** Having something to eat every three or four hours will prevent your blood sugar from getting low and dragging your mood down with it.
- **Eat wisely (carbohydrates).** Your body gets most of its energy from carbohydrates, such as sugars, starch, and fiber. Sugary foods and other simple carbs give you a quick burst of energy but break down very quickly in your body, so your blood sugar and mood plummet soon after eating. Complex carbs like whole grains, fruits, and vegetables are digested more slowly. In addition, carbohydrates may help improve serotonin levels in your brain.
- **Eat wisely (B vitamins).** Low levels of folic acid (vitamin B_9) and vitamin B_{12} may contribute to depression. Good sources of B vitamins include oranges and other citrus fruits, leafy green vegetables, beans, and eggs.
- **Drink water.** Make sure to drink even before you feel thirsty so you don't get dehydrated.

Exercise

Physical activity is one of the best things you can do for your overall health. Along with strengthening your muscles and bones and reducing your risk of diabetes and other diseases, it can distract you from your problems, lower your stress level, help you sleep more soundly, boost your self-esteem, and improve your mood.

Regular exercise can be great for your self-confidence, especially when you see improvement—like when you realize that the heavy weights you started training with are now light. If you run, signing up for a race can give you a specific goal to work toward; there are "couch to 5K" (or longer) training plans available online to motivate you. If you enjoy team sports, you might be able to find an informal game at a nearby park.

But you don't have to be good at sports to increase your physical activity. Try climbing the stairs instead of using the elevator, or walk around while you're talking on the phone. Even playing fetch with your dog can make your heart beat faster and elevate your mood.

GET ACTIVE

The best kind of exercise is any exercise you stick with. These tips can help turn exercise into a habit:

- **Do something you enjoy.** If it's fun, it won't seem like a chore.
- **Ask a friend to join you.** Setting up a regular time to exercise with a buddy will help keep you committed.
- **Do something physical most days of the week.** Short but frequent workouts are better for you than long but rare ones. Even 10 minutes of activity every day can make a difference.
- **Don't worry if you miss a day.** Sometimes you may not have time to exercise—just do your best to fit it in tomorrow.
- **Listen to something interesting.** If you get bored easily, find entertaining music, podcasts, or audiobooks for when you work out.
- **Be proud.** You're taking a big step to improve yourself.

Sleep

According to the National Sleep Foundation, teenagers should get 8 to 10 hours of sleep every night. But a study published in 2010 found that nearly 70 percent of U.S. high school students get less than 7 hours of sleep on an average school night.

In addition to making you tired and cranky, lack of sleep can mess with your physical and mental health. Fatigue makes it harder to deal with stressful situations and increases your risk of depression. Giving your body the time it needs to rest and recover makes it easier to face everyday challenges.

Here are some tips to improve your sleep:

- **Get a consistent amount of sleep.** This means every night, even on weekends.

Taking devices to bed with you is not a good idea. The light from the screen confuses your body, and activities like texting or playing games can make it hard to relax.

- **Develop a bedtime routine.** Doing the same things lets your body know that it should be winding down for the night.
- **Adjust your computer and phone screens.** Blue light coming from electronic displays can interfere with your body's production of melatonin, the hormone that signals that it's time to go to sleep. Use an app that automatically adjusts the brightness and color of your screens during the day to cut down that light and help your natural sleep cycle.
- **Put down electronic devices an hour before bedtime.** It's easy to lose track of time when you're looking at Instagram or texting with friends, so put away your devices and let your brain relax.
- **Talk to your doctor about a melatonin supplement.** Taking melatonin within a couple of hours of bedtime can help inform your body that the day is ending.
- **Avoid caffeine in the evening.** This includes coffee, tea, some soft drinks and energy drinks, and chocolate.
- **Use your bed just for sleeping.** Do other activities away from your bedroom so your brain doesn't associate it with staying awake.
- **Streamline your morning routine.** If you shower and choose your outfit for school the night before, you can get up a bit later.

Building Resilience

Certain people are better than others at getting through challenging experiences. They have resilience, or the ability to bounce back from difficult situations. Even when things look bleak, they're able to remain flexible and adapt to change.

Being resilient doesn't mean you never fail or experience setbacks—it means you're able to cope when they occur. It gives you strong defenses to get through whatever bad things happen. Kids with high self-esteem tend to be more resilient because their belief in their abilities helps them cope with stressful situations.

BUILDING SELF-ESTEEM

Kids with mood or anxiety disorders often have low self-esteem. As their condition improves, their self-esteem typically does as well. But actively working to improve your opinion of yourself can give you a jump start. Here are some ideas:

- **Try new activities.** You'll boost your self-confidence and might even find a new hobby.
- **Be proud of your accomplishments.** Make a list of achievements or put reminders up where you'll see them.
- **Change negative thoughts into positive ones.** We're often more critical of ourselves than we would be of others. Be generous to yourself and remember all your amazing qualities.
- **Schedule time to do things you enjoy.** Write an activity you like to do on each day of your calendar and stick to your plan every day.
- **Speak up.** Express yourself and be assertive.
- **Set reasonable goals.** Don't push too fast so you don't get discouraged.
- **Spend time with people who make you feel good.** If certain friends make you feel worse about yourself, you're better off without them.

You can develop resilience to help you cope with future challenges. These suggestions may help:

- **Recognize that change is inevitable.** Figure out how you can adapt to the new circumstances.

- **Take a small step forward.** It's tempting to just give up when things look rough. Instead, try to identify a realistic next move to improve your situation, even if you can't fix it completely.
- **Learn from your misfortunes.** Getting through hardships teaches you about yourself and helps you grow and develop greater self-respect.
- **Be confident in your skills.** Trust your abilities and have faith that you'll find a way to deal with your problems.
- **Look at the big picture.** Events that feel like tragedies right now may seem minor when you look back on them later. Years from now, nobody will remember that one test you failed.
- **Try to be hopeful.** Think about how you're going to reach your goals, rather than wasting time on what worries you.

Dealing with Everyday Stress

No matter how good your life is, you're going to face stress from school, family, friends, and other sources. In the short term, stress can be beneficial, because it pushes you to do your best. But if you're constantly stressed, you might start to feel overwhelmed.

Long-term or severe stress can cause physical symptoms like headaches, stomachaches, tense muscles, and trouble sleeping, as well as trouble concentrating. It can also make depression or anxiety worse.

If you recognize that you're getting overwhelmed, you can manage it before it's out of hand.

EDUCATIONAL VIDEO

Scan this code for a video about self-esteem.

In addition to the tips above, here are a few more strategies to help you through stressful times:

- **Hang out with friends.** You may want to hide away from everyone, but getting together with others is one of the best ways to take your mind off things.

- **Talk to someone.** Whether it's a friend, a school counselor, or some other trusted adult, speak with someone about how you're feeling. They can give you a different perspective and help you work through small problems before they turn into big ones.

- **Take breaks.** Step away from the textbooks or computer and just chill out for a while: listen to music, read a magazine, or close your eyes and imagine your dream vacation.

- **Keep a journal.** Whenever you feel tense or upset, take some time to write about it. Venting your feelings might help you figure out how to deal with the situation better next time.

THE TROUBLE WITH SOCIAL MEDIA

If you spend a lot of time on social media, you may start to feel as though everyone has a perfect life but you. All those posts bragging about accomplishments and photos of fabulous vacations can set impossibly high standards. But when you look at your friends' feeds, keep in mind that most people are posting only their highlights. They're selecting what they show the world and editing out their struggles and failures. If you recognize that, you might feel less envious.

Consider taking a vacation from social media. It can be hard to feel like you're missing out on what's happening, but you may find that you worry less about comparing yourself to others.

Some days you might feel like retreating, but try to let friends help you. Support is important.

- **Work on a hobby.** Drawing, writing poetry, and playing guitar are all activities that can make you feel less stressed. Don't worry about creating a masterpiece—just express yourself.
- **Do something for others.** Find somewhere to volunteer in your community, like at the public library or a community center.

Maintaining Friendships

When you have a mood or anxiety disorder, it can be hard to maintain friendships, but it's worth it to make the effort. Don't wait for your friends to call you; reach out to them to make plans to do something fun—even just window-shopping in town. Remember that your friends may be busy with their own activities, so don't take it to heart if they're not available. Try to make plans in advance so they're not already busy when you call.

Friends are an important part of getting through difficult times, and it can be a relief to be open about what you're going through. Good friends accept you as you are, even if they don't always understand everything about you. In the end, it's your decision who to tell. Writing down the pros and cons of telling different people can help you decide who's likely to be most supportive.

Trying to make new friends can be intimidating at any time, and even more so when you'd rather just stay at home by yourself. But good friends are a vital part of your support system. The easiest way to meet new potential friends is to participate in activities you already enjoy—it could be reading graphic novels, painting still lifes, or playing kickball. See whether there's a neighborhood or community interest group you can join that meets regularly. Your school or local

You don't need to be the most popular kid in school; having a buddy who understands you can be enough.

community organizations might host after-school groups, or you could look online (such as the site www.meetup.com) for listings in your area.

When a Friend Is Depressed

At some point you may notice that a good friend seems withdrawn or is acting much differently than usual. This may just be a passing problem, but it could be an early sign of a mental health condition. Here are a few ways you can show your support:

EDUCATIONAL VIDEO

Scan this code for a video with advice for supporting friends with mental disorders.

- Suggest that they go talk to a doctor or the school counselor to get help. If they're scared or don't feel up to it, offer to go with them or to contact a trusted adult yourself.
- Support their treatment. Remind them that treatment will help them get better.
- Be patient and find ways to show that you care about them, like calling or texting regularly just to check in.
- Read about their condition so you get a better idea of what they're going through.
- Ask what you can do to help. Offer specific ideas, like sharing your class notes from days when they miss school.
- Invite them to do things with you. If they say no, accept their answer, but keep inviting them to other activities so they know you're thinking of them.
- Keep their personal information confidential. Just because they trusted you doesn't mean they want others to know.

- If they talk about suicide, ask them to call the National Suicide Prevention Lifeline at 1-800-273-TALK (8255). Call 911 if you think there's an immediate risk that they'll hurt themselves. Be sure to tell someone else you trust.

What to Say and What Not to Say

You wouldn't say, "It's all in your head" to someone with diabetes, but that kind of comment is made all the time to people with depression and anxiety. Remember that mental disorders are real, and people can't just "get over it."

It can be tricky to find the right thing to say to show your support. Even though you're trying to help, avoid statements like "Look on the bright side" or "Everyone feels like this sometimes." Instead, let your friend know that you're there to support him or her. The following are examples of nonjudgmental statements you can use:

- I want you to know that I care about you.
- I don't understand exactly what you're going through, but I'm here to help if I can.
- You're not alone. You mean a lot to me.
- You can get through this. The right treatment will help you start feeling better.

Text-Dependent Questions

1. Why is whole-grain bread better for your mood than white bread?
2. How does using your phone right before bedtime disrupt your sleep?
3. In what way can stress be useful?

Research Project

Many articles have been published about the effects of exercise on depression and anxiety disorders. Find a recent study on this subject. Describe the methods used, the main results, and the conclusions reached by the authors.

FURTHER READING

Erika's Lighthouse. "The Toolbox." http://www.erikaslighthouse.org/the-toolbox.

Hand, Carol. *Living with Depression.* Minneapolis, MN: ABDO, 2014.

Miller, Allen R. *Living with Anxiety Disorders.* New York: Facts on FIle, 2008.

MedlinePlus. "Teen Mental Health." https://medlineplus.gov/teenmentalhealth. html.

TeenMentalHealth.org. "Learn." http://teenmentalhealth.org/learn/.

Tompkins, Michael A., and Katherine A. Martinez. *My Anxious Mind: A Teen's Guide to Managing Anxiety and Panic.* Washington, DC: Magination Press, 2010.

Zucker, Bonnie. *Take Control of OCD: The Ultimate Guide for Kids With OCD.* Waco, TX: Prufrock Press, 2011.

Educational Videos

Chapter One: TEDxYouth. "Insight into the Teenage Brain: Adriana Galván at TEDxYouth@Caltech." https://youtu.be/LWUkW4s3XxY.

Chapter Two: CrashCourse. "Depressive and Bipolar Disorders: Crash Course Psychology #30." https://youtu.be/ZwMlHkWKDwM.

Chapter Three: HowStuffWorks."Shy vs. Social Anxiety." https://youtu.be/ We6U-KrJ6E4.

Chapter Four: Kati Morton. "What Is a Treatment Plan & How Do We Make One? Mental Health Help with Kati Morton." https://youtu.be/K4fbZvME1fI.

Chapter Five: TEDxYouth. "Meet Yourself: A User's Guide to Building Self-Esteem: Niko Everett at TEDxYouth@BommerCanyon." https://youtu.be/ uOrzmFUJtrs.

Chapter Five: Julia Kristina Counseling. "Love Someone Who Has Depression? This is What You Need to Know." https://youtu.be/k5PRxE4yJpw.

SERIES GLOSSARY

accommodation: an arrangement or adjustment to a new situation; for example, schools make accommodations to help students cope with illness.

anemia: an illness caused by a lack of red blood cells.

autoimmune: type of disorder where the body's immune system attacks the body's tissues instead of germs.

benign: not harmful.

biofeedback: a technique used to teach someone how to control some bodily functions.

capillaries: tiny blood vessels that carry blood from larger blood vessels to body tissues.

carcinogens: substances that can cause cancer to develop.

cerebellum: the back part of the brain; it controls movement.

cerebrum: the front part of the brain; it controls many higher-level thinking and functions.

cholesterol: a waxy substance associated with fats that coats the inside of blood vessels, causing cardiovascular disease.

cognitive: related to conscious mental activities, such as learning and thinking.

communicable: transferable from one person to another.

congenital: a condition or disorder that exists from birth.

correlation: a connection between different things that suggests they may have something to do with one another.

dominant: in genetics, a dominant trait is expressed in a child even when the trait is only inherited from one parent.

environmental factors: anything that affects how people live, develop, or grow. Climate, diet, and pollution are examples.

genes: units of hereditary information.

hemorrhage: bleeding from a broken blood vessel.

hormones: substances the body produces to instruct cells and tissues to perform certain actions.

inflammation: redness, swelling, and tenderness in a part of the body in response to infection or injury.

insulin: a hormone produced in the pancreas that controls cells' ability to absorb glucose.

lymphatic system: part of the human immune system; transports white blood cells around the body.

malignant: harmful; relating to tumors, likely to spread.

mutation: a change in the structure of a gene; some mutations are harmless, but others may cause disease.

neurological: relating to the nervous system (including the brain and spinal cord).

neurons: specialized cells found in the central nervous system (the brain and spinal cord).

occupational therapy: a type of therapy that teaches one how to accomplish tasks and activities in daily life.

oncology: the study of cancer.

orthopedic: dealing with deformities in bones or muscles.

prevalence: how common or uncommon a disease is in any given population.

prognosis: the forecast for the course of a disease that predicts whether a person with the disease will get sicker, recover, or stay the same.

progressive disease: a disease that generally gets worse as time goes on.

psychomotor: relating to movement or muscle activity resulting from mental activity.

recessive: in genetics, a recessive trait will only be expressed if a child inherits it from both parents.

remission: an improvement in or disappearance of someone's symptoms of disease; unlike a cure, remission is usually temporary.

resilience: the ability to bounce back from difficult situations.

seizure: an event caused by unusual brain activity resulting in physical or behavior changes.

syndrome: a condition with a set of associated symptoms.

ulcers: a break or sore in skin or tissue where cells disintegrate and die. Infections may occur at the site of an ulcer.

INDEX

Illlustrations are indicated by page numbers in *italic* type.

ABOUT THE ADVISOR

Heather Pelletier, Ph.D., is a pediatric staff psychologist at Rhode Island Hospital/Hasbro Children's Hospital with a joint appointment as a clinical assistant professor in the departments of Psychiatry and Human Behavior and Pediatrics at the Warren Alpert Medical School of Brown University. She is also the director of behavioral pain medicine in the division of Children's Integrative therapies, Pain management and Supportive care (CHIPS) in the department of Pediatrics at Hasbro Children's Hospital. Dr. Pelletier provides clinical services to children in various medical specialty clinics at Hasbro Children's Hospital, including the pediatric gastroenterology, nutrition, and liver disease clinics.

ABOUT THE AUTHOR

Andrea Balinson is a writer and editor of educational materials for patients and health care professionals. She has helped develop 3D animations showing how various drugs work within the human body, as well as videos and multimedia exhibits presented at medical conferences. In addition, she has contributed to training manuals and reports for wildlife conservation and animal welfare organizations.

PHOTO CREDITS